D.O.DOUBLE G

Published in 2024 by OH!
An Imprint of Welbeck Non-Fiction Limited,
part of Welbeck Publishing Group.
Offices in: London – 20 Mortimer Street, London W1T 3JW
and Sydney – Level 17, 207 Kent St, Sydney NSW 2000 Australia
www.welbeckpublishing.com

ISBN 978-1-80069-627-3

Compiled and written by: Malcolm Croft
Editorial: Victoria Denne
Project manager: Russell Porter
Production: Rachel Burgess

A CIP catalogue record for this book is available from the British Library

Printed in Dubai

10 9 8 7 6 5 4 3 2 1

D.O.DOUBLE G

THE LITTLE GUIDE TO
SNOOP DOGG

CONTENTS

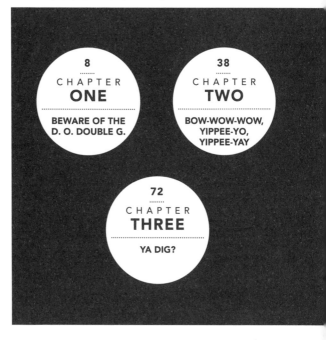

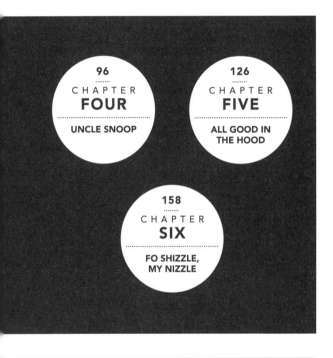

INTRODUCTION

Welcome to the world's greatest doggography, a bookizzle dedicated solely to the slick wisecrackin' of the doggfather of hip-hop – Snoop Dogg!

Strap in, because this candid collection of quotes is about to plug itself directly into the genius-level brain of "America's most lovable pimp", and things are going to get a little dizzle to the hizzle, fo shizzle.

In 1992, Snoop – a gangbangin', drug pimpin', joint-jumpin' rapper from America's most notorious hood – emerged from the streets of Long Beach, California, as Dr. Dre's first protegé on his 1992 masterpiece, *The Chronic*. His mentor predicted even then that "Snoop is the biggest thing to happen to Black people since the straightening comb". How right he was.

When Snoop dropped his debut, *Doggystyle*, a year later, it got West Coast gangstas paid from the mainstream: white Middle America. With producer Dr. Dre, Snoop lit the spark for many other rappers to find fame and fortune and, ever since, has pushed the boundaries of what's possible for a street-born-and-raised hoodlum, building a global apparel empire (all available on his online Snoopermarket) while also marketing his own brand of dogma too: peace, love and weed.

Today, Snoop is the granduncle of the hip-hop scene, remaining its most influential star, and an essential icon of popular culture – as gifted in the studio booth as he is in the boardroom. This tiny tome takes the D. O. double G off his leash for a long walk down memory lane, digging up the bones of his earliest and most recent interviews and chewing on the truth bombs that only Snoop Doggizzle can lay down – all under one roof. (Or woof, if you prefer.)

From killer quotes to classic quips, life philosophy to personal beliefs, this little guide is all you need to stay up to speed about the world's first OG turned elder statesman… and the only way to celebrate over 30 years of *Doggystyle* without putting your back out.

Enjoy!

CHAPTER
ONE

BEWARE OF THE D.O.DOUBLE G

Snoop may have made the journey from the streets of Long Beach, California, to worldwide fame and fortune seem all too easy, but his road to success was full of chasing cars and chronic chaos.

From murder charges to multiple felony arrests, gang bustin' to drive-by shootings, Snoop's course correction from ending up on Death Row records is now nuthin' but a G thang. Welcome to Doggyland…

66

You can take me out of the ghetto, but you can't take the ghetto out of me.

99

Snoop, on his ghetto roots, interview with David Sheff, *Playboy*, October 1, 1995.

66

When I rapped in the hallways at school, I would draw such a big crowd that the principal would think there was a fight going on. It made me begin to realize that I had a gift. I could tell that my raps interested people and that made me interested in myself.

99

Snoop, on his earliest rapping days at school, interview with Chuck Philips, *LA Times*, November 7, 1993.

"

When I was a small boy, if we had a problem, we would fight about it with our fists. We wouldn't shoot somebody, killing them or wounding them. That's not hard to do. I would like people to put down the guns. If you have a problem, talk about it.

"

Snoop, on solving conflicts as a youngster, interview with David Sheff, *Playboy*, October 1, 1995.

66

My momma gave me the name Snoop. I used to love *Peanuts* and *Charlie Brown* – Snoopy was my favorite cartoon character growing up. I watched so much, I started to look like him.

99

Snoop, on the origin of his moniker, interview with Mike Sager, *Esquire*, July 14, 2008.

The name "Snoop" was given to Calvin Cordozar Broadus Jr. by his mother Beverly Tate, after the *Peanuts* cartoon dog, Snoopy.

The "Doggy Dogg" part of this stage moniker was borrowed from his cousin, Tate Doggy Dog.

"

When I decided to call myself Snoop Doggy Dogg, Tate didn't much like it, but I said to him, 'Tate, I'm gonna take this name to the stars' and I did.

"

Snoop, on his Doggy Dog name, interview with Chuck Philips, *LA Times*, November 7, 1993.

66

In jail, you're either gonna be the toughest motherfucker, or you gonna be the softest motherfucker... or you gotta find some other shit to be.

99

Snoop, on what he learnt from his time spent in jail (following his drug bust), interview with Mike Sager, *Esquire*, July 14, 2008.

66

I went to a white elementary school, but they accepted you if you were a Black gifted athlete from the inner city. They had gymnastics, swimming, track and field, music classes – all this shit we weren't getting in the hood. It showed me how to interact with white people. When I started making music, it wasn't a surprise to me that white people loved my music as much as Black people because I knew how to relate.

99

Snoop, on his upbringing, interview with Mike Sager, *Esquire*, July 14, 2008.

66

In prison the older inmates would tell me I was too talented to be in there. I was like, why would they tell me this? They're doin' time, and they don't give a fuck about me. For them to overlook all that shit, it showed that I had a gift, so I figured I had to use it to the fullest.

99

Snoop, on his cellmates as fans, interview with Steven Daly, *The Face*, February 1994.

"

I've been shot at plenty of times. Drive-bys, walk-bys. It ain't like that *Boyz n the Hood* shit. It's worse. In the movie, you know it's going to come, because of the music or the scene before. On the streets, you don't get scenes. You could be hanging out, holding your baby, and talking to your mama, and a car will ride up real slow. You ain't even paying attention, and they serve y'all. You, your baby, and your mom.

"

Snoop, on being shot at, interview with David Sheff, *Playboy*, October 1, 1995.

60 per cent

The number of rhymes written and rapped by Snoop on Dr. Dre's seminal 1992 masterpiece, *The Chronic*, the largest contribution by a single rapper by far.

This record was Snoop's first taste of success and sold more than 6 million copies.

66

They just dropped off guns and drugs and gave us a path to destruction. And then they locked us all up.

99

Snoop, on the government and CIA's activities in the 1980s in Black neighbourhoods, interview with Lyndsey Parker, *Yahoo Music*, May 10, 2021.

66

I was supposed to go to the penitentiary on the first violation [of possession of cocaine for sale], but he just sent me to the county jail to get my life together. In the county you might get stabbed or something; but in the pen, you could die.

99

Snoop, on his first stint in county jail, interview with Steven Daly, *The Face*, February 1994.

66

Dre's half-brother, Warren G, was in my group, 213 – me, him, and Nate Dogg. And we had a cassette tape and Warren G took it to Dr. Dre's bachelor party. And the music had cut off from the bachelor party. So, Warren G slipped my tape in, and people started dancing to it. And Dre was like 'Who is that?' Warren G was like, 'That's my homeboy, Snoop.' He introduced me to Dre… and the rest is history.

99

Snoop, on meeting Dr. Dre for the first time, interview with Larry King, *Larry King Live CNN*, March 26, 2010.

"

I was like the class clown in school so I guess I would say I did like the attention. In church I did a lot of plays, my mother made me play characters, do a lot of drama and acting, trying to become someone else. So, it helped me create who I am, to create Snoop Dogg.

"

Snoop, on his formative years and love of performance, interview with Elizabeth Day, *The Guardian*, June 19, 2011.

February 20, 1996

The date Snoop, and his bodyguard McKinley Lee, were acquitted of first- and second-degree murder following the shooting of Philip Woldermariam, a member of a rival gang. Snoop was the driver of the vehicle from which shots were fired.

The two-year trial began while Snoop was recording his debut album, *Doggystyle*.

66

In Bel Air and Beverly Hills, 90 per cent of the babies get taken care of. In the ghettos, it's 15 per cent. Kids don't learn. It starts in the home. A mother and father or no father or mother. Nobody lays out a foundation of how shit is supposed to be. The pattern goes on.

99

Snoop, on the vicious cycle of ghetto life, interview with David Sheff, *Playboy*, October 1, 1995.

"

In the 80s era of drugs and gang violence, to see 21 years old was a blessing. That's what we were always striving to, to actually make 21. To see 21 meant a lot to my era, to my generation, because a lot of us wasn't making it to that number.

"

Snoop, on turning 21, interview by Lyndsey Parker, *Yahoo Music*, May 10, 2021.

"

I don't see too many ways out. I know Black people in my neighborhood who had straight A's, but who couldn't get into college because their families didn't have no finances. So, what are they supposed to do? Go work at McDonald's makin' $4.35 an hour? They're supposed to cheat themselves like that? They're not makin' it easy for us at all.

"

Snoop, on America's broken employment system, interview with Steven Daly, *The Face*, February 1994.

"

I always had my own little style in school. My voice was real light, like a girl, and I could just hear some music and make up raps about whatever was takin' place. Whenever I had to challenge somebody, I would beat 'em. I could work the crowd real smooth because I was so little.

"

Snoop, on rapping at high school and his signature style, interview with Steven Daly, *The Face*, February 1994.

66

When I got arrested,
I thought that was wrong,
crazy shit. I didn't understand.
How could I go to jail for
selling some drugs?

99

Snoop, on his arrest, aged 18, for cocaine dealing,
interview with David Sheff, *Playboy*, October 1, 1995.

66

I could beat 'em all. And this showed me: man, this is something I need to be doing because it's so easy for me and these guys were staying up all night writing songs and I'm just saying whatever's on my mind, right there on the spot, and it's better than what they're doing so maybe it's my calling to do this.

99

Snoop, on his high-school hip-hop battles, aged 15, interview with Elizabeth Day, *The Guardian*, June 19, 2011.

"

I'm going to grow in this game because I'm a student, I don't dwell on the past. I don't even listen to *The Chronic* no more, and soon I won't listen to *Doggystyle* because I'll be ready to turn to the next page. It's too early to get caught up in the success of my album because I haven't done anything yet.

"

Snoop, on always looking to the future, interview with Steven Daly, *The Face*, February 1994.

66

I'm going to try to eliminate the gang violence. I'll be on a mission for peace. I know I have a lot of power. I know if I say, 'Don't kill', they won't kill.

99

Snoop, on his power and purpose to promote gun control, interview with Touré, *New York Times*, November 21, 1993.

> **"**
> Shante has been by my side
> since before I was Snoop.
> I was rapping to get her
> feedback on my songs before
> anyone would listen.
> **"**

Snoop, on his wife, Shante, interview with *Vanity Fair*, January 28, 2022.

66

They thought Crippin' was bad.
I taught them that Crippin'
was fashionable.

99

Snoop, on the Crips, his former L.A. gang, interview with
Elliott Wilson, *CRWN*, August 8, 2016.

"

What people don't understand is joining a gang ain't bad, it's cool. Because all your friends are in the gang, all your family's in the gang. We're not just killing people every night; we're hanging out and having a good time. So, it's like, it's more a family than anything, and it's easier to become a family than it is to get a job.

"

Snoop, on being a member of the Crips, an L.A. gang, interview with Elizabeth Day, *The Guardian*, June 19, 2011.

66

I thought I was going to go down for murder… When you're in court, you have no real sense of vibe and what is going to be until they read it off. You're in there trying to be on your best behaviour, they're tearing your character down, they're bringing up pictures of you with guns, and the kind of person you were when you were that person, and saying you're still that person, and you're on that witness stand and you can't even say anything.

99

Snoop, on his two-year murder trial in 1996, interview with Simon Hattenstone, *The Guardian*, April 6, 2013.

CHAPTER
TWO

BOW-WOW-WOW, YIPPEE-YO, YIPPEE-YAY

The next episode of Snoop's life was straight outta Hollywood, a fairy tale that no one could have seen coming.

Gangbanger turned bona fide rap sensation, Snoop's arrival on the West Coast scene elevated gangsta rap to the world's new favourite soundtrack. And Snoop's special brand of *Doggystyle* was leading the pack…

66

Doggystyle is about what I grew up with, what I been through, what goes on today. It's just everyday life, if it didn't happen, I couldn't make money off it. If this shit didn't occur, there wouldn't be no people buyin' it.

99

Snoop, on his debut 1993 album *Doggystyle*, interview with Paul Lester, *The Guardian*, July 3, 1994.

To date, Snoop has sold more than 37 million albums worldwide.

His debut, *Doggystyle*, remains his biggest hit, selling more than 6 million copies.

> **"**
>
> I wanted to be a gangsta my whole life. Even when I came home from church, we'd see all the gangstas and that was more appealing to me, so when I finally got a chance to live it, to do it, I rapped about it. I was like, 'I'm going to do it like nobody's ever done it before because my shit is going to be 100 per cent authentic because I come from it, and I am it.'
>
> **"**

Snoop, on gangsta life as influence, interview with Simon Hattenstone, *The Guardian*, April 6, 2013.

66

I deal with shit nobody
else has done before. Not
even Elvis.

99

Snoop, on his fame, celebrity and ubiquity, interview with
Paul Lester, *Melody Maker*, February 5, 1994.

"

One thing about a hit is this –
you can't deny a hit when you
hear it. You know it's a hit and
you gonna roll with it like that.
Every hit I ever done; I knew it
was gonna be a smash.

"

Snoop, on his biggest hit songs, interview with
Clash Magazine, January 2009.

66

I would like my critics to spend one week in the neighbourhood I grew up in, and then maybe they'll understand. I'm just speakin' real.

99

Snoop, on detractors of gangsta rap, interview with Paul Lester, *Melody Maker*, February 5, 1994.

"

That shit is crazy!
Ain't nobody else bigger than
me but Michael Jackson.

"

Snoop, on being America's newest music star, interview
with Paul Lester, *Melody Maker*, February 5, 1994.

66

I didn't make up the word 'bitch'. There were bitches before 1992!

99

Snoop, on his (over) use of negative stereotypes in his lyrics, interview with *Clash Magazine*, 1995.

66

I really don't understand women exactly, to be real with ya. But I do respect all women, on the whole.

99

Snoop, on the fairer sex, interview by
Paul Lester, *Melody Maker*, February 5, 1994.

Snoop has appeared, as both a leading character and cameo, in more than 30 films. His best-known roles are in the following:

1. *Training Day*
2. *Old School*
3. *Starsky and Hutch*
4. *Scary Movie 5*
5. *Turbo*
6. *Pitch Perfect 2*
7. *Popstar: Never Stop Popping*
8. *The Beach Bum*
9. *House Party*
10. *Dolemite is My Name*

66

I'm a rapper putting words together from a basic education level. I'm not complicated at all. I say raps that your two-year-old son can learn.

99

Snoop, on his unique rap style, interview with David Sheff, *Playboy*, October 1, 1995.

"

Drugs came into our neighbourhood.
And once the drugs became part
of our life, guns were introduced to
us, and once you introduce the guns
and drugs, it becomes jealousy and
protect your neighbourhood, and
before you know it somebody gets
shot at, and you do the shooting.
And it just goes on and on.

"

Snoop, on the vicious ghetto cycle of violence, interview
with Simon Hattenstone, *The Guardian*, April 6, 2013.

66

I want to become a young Black entrepreneur, a businessman, leader of the youth and for my music to have a positive message behind it. In the future, my music is going to be containing a much clearer positive message, but it will be just as real.

99

Snoop, on his global domination intentions, interview with *Clash Magazine*, 1995.

"

You think my music is sellout music? Listen. I've put out only one album. When I'm through and put my Barry White collection of albums together, motherfuckers will respect me. Worldwide. This is just volume one. There's more to come.

"

Snoop, on selling 4 million records on his debut album and his plans for world domination, interview with David Sheff, *Playboy*, October 1, 1995.

> **"**
>
> That shit was scary 'cos I just turned 18. But I didn't cry myself to sleep or nothin'. You can't show no weakness, 'cos then you'll be stuck. You gotta handle yourself like a professional.
>
> **"**

Snoop, on being sent to jail aged 18, interview with Paul Lester, *Melody Maker*, February 5, 1994.

66

The hardass gangbanger life ain't the bomb at all, period. The other day I was looking at an old picture from back when I used to play football, and, like, of twenty-eight homies on the team, twelve are dead, seven are in the penitentiary, three of them are smoke out and only me and Warren G are successful. I love my homies, but damn, I don't want to stay down there with y'all.

99

Snoop, on getting out of the ghetto, interview with Jeff Rosenthal, *Rolling Stone*, July 31, 2012.

"

The little Black kids are saying, 'Well, damn! Snoop Dogg comes from the same neck of the woods we do, and he made it and he's able to say what he wants to say. I want to be like him.' That's the dream right there.

"

Snoop, on being an inspiration for others to better their beginnings, interview with David Sheff, *Playboy*, October 1, 1995.

January 31, 2001

The date Snoop released Snoop Dogg's *Doggystyle*, a mix of hardcore pornography and hip-hop music videos presented by him and featuring his music. Snoop does not, ahem, perform in the movie.

It was the first hardcore film to make the *Billboard* music video sales chart and spawned a trend of countless imitations in the rap community. The movie was even filmed at Snoop's house in Claremont, California.

> **"**
> I brought the situation of the ghettos to the attention of the people who would not have known or cared otherwise. That's all I'm doing. People forget that they were told about the wars. They only know because someone sat around and talked about it.
> **"**

Snoop, on rapping about the realities of the ghettos, interview with *Clash Magazine*, 1995.

"

So, me and Dre became best friends. We were like one-two punch, the way Suge Knight and Tupac were, that's how me and Dre were every day for real, though.

"

Snoop, on Dr. Dre, interview by Elliott Wilson, *GQ*, December 8, 2021.

❝

Clint Eastwood, Charles Bronson – they can kill a million motherfuckers in their movies and create bad images for the kids, but once they get off the screen everybody praises them and loves them. But when we do our art in my studio, we get criticized for it, rather than let it go for what it is – confession. You'd never sweat Charles Bronson about havin' no gun, so why you are sweatin' me?

❞

Snoop, on the double standards in culture and gangsta rap, interview with Paul Lester, *Melody Maker*, February 5, 1994.

> **"**
> I was popular as fuck in
> school. I was fun to be around.
> Motherfuckers loved me for
> my rap, they loved me because
> I made them laugh.
> **"**

Snoop, on being popular at high school, interview with
David Sheff, *Playboy*, October 1, 1995.

Snoop's biggest hit single remains "Gin and Juice", the second single from *Doggystyle*. The song samples "I Get Lifted" by KC and The Sunshine Band.

In 2018, Snoop broke the Guinness World Record for "World's Biggest Gin and Juice" when he stirred up a cocktail that contained 180 bottles of gin, 154 bottles of apricot brandy and 38 jugs of orange juice.

66

There ain't nothing a young man can do to prepare himself for the hell I've gone through. I'm living positive. I've been through jail. I've been through selling drugs. I've been shot at. But I'm just as cool as ever. I don't understand the big misperception that people feel I'm a villain or something – I'm no sort of roughneck. I'm a smooth macadamia.

99

Snoop, on his ghetto gangbanging life before fame, interview with Jonathan Gold, *SPIN*, February 1997.

"

In jail, I got respect from my rapping. I was rapping every motherfucking night. I rapped about whatever the fuck was going on. Whatever we ate that day. I would ask other prisoners about some shit that happened in their hood, and I would put it down in rap form. Some of that shit ended up on Dre's album.

"

Snoop, on honing his rapping style in jail, interview with David Sheff, *Playboy*, October 1, 1995.

66

Tonight, I'm writing a letter to the District Attorney. I'ma tell him, 'Sorry. You can't have me.'

99

Snoop, outside an L.A. courthouse, after being acquitted of first- and second-degree murder following a two-year trial, *SPIN*, February 1997.

66

> Growing up I didn't dream of living in the ghetto my whole life. I wanted to get out. I'm not trying to run from the hood, I'm just trying to have expectations and goals to get the finer things in life. That's all.

Snoop, on getting out of the hood, interview with David Sheff, *Playboy*, October 1, 1995.

66

Too much talent on one team can be bad. There's just so much dopeness you can put on a record, and when everyone becomes such a superstar, they don't listen anymore: 'Motherfucker, I sold three million records. You can't be telling me what to do.'

99

Snoop, on splitting from Dr. Dre, after *Doggystyle*'s success in 1993, interview with Jonathan Gold, *SPIN*, February 1997.

In a career that has spanned more than 30 years, Snoop has remained prolific, releasing 20 studio albums:

1. *Doggystyle* (1993)
2. *Tha Doggfather* (1996)
3. *Da Game Is to Be Sold, Not to Be Told* (1998)
4. *No Limit Top Dogg* (1999)
5. *Tha Last Meal* (2000)
6. *Paid tha Cost to Be da Boss* (2002)
7. *R&G (Rhythm & Gangsta): The Masterpiece* (2004)
8. *Tha Blue Carpet Treatment* (2006)
9. *Ego Trippin'* (2008)
10. *Malice n Wonderland* (2009)
11. *Doggumentary* (2011)
12. *Reincarnated* (2013)
13. *Bush* (2015)
14. *Coolaid* (2016)
15. *Neva Left* (2017)
16. *Bible of Love* (2018)
17. *I Wanna Thank Me* (2019)
18. *From tha Streets 2 tha Suites* (2021)
19. *BODR* (2022)
20. *Missionary* (2024)

> **"**
>
> I could get that East Coast/ West Coast bullshit stopped, get the most powerful rappers from the East, and get a peace treaty going. We could get into the studio together and show the world that Black men can pull together for peace. Then we can move on and make some money.
>
> **"**

Snoop, on squashing the East/West Coast beefs, interview with Jonathan Gold, *SPIN*, February 1997.

66

As a Black man, I have to respect myself and have nice things. As a man in general. If they would have put positive opportunities in front of me to make $1000 a week, I would have done it. But they didn't. They put $1000 in front of me and an illegal way to make it.

99

Snoop, on the failing job and welfare system for Black men in the ghetto, interview with David Sheff, *Playboy*, October 1, 1995.

"

Dre's *Chronic* album, which I participated on, goes to levels that people never thought such a hard rap album could go to. It ain't like he just put me on there. I deserved that shit because I worked hard. It sounded good, me and him together.

"

Snoop, on Dr. Dre's *The Chronic*, interview with David Sheff, *Playboy*, October 1, 1995.

CHAPTER
THREE

YA DIG?

Flushed with success from heavy MTV rotation of "Gin and Juice" and "Murder Was the Case", Snoop was on top of the world, despite a noose hanging over his head for his now-infamous two-year murder trial.

Never before had America – the world, too – celebrated such a controversy-courting character (who wasn't white) and soon to be beloved as *tha Doggfather* of hip-hop. Ya dig?

"

For little kids growing up in the ghettos, it's easy to get into gangbanging and selling drugs. I've seen what that was like, and I don't glorify it, but I don't preach. I feel like it's my job to play the backup role for parents who can't get it across to their kids. I bring it to them rather than have them go find out about it for themselves.

"

Snoop, on inspiring young ghetto kids, interview with Touré, *New York Times*, January 17, 2008.

" The media created the buzz of gangsta rap being so terrible, but terrible is the ghetto shit we write about. Violence happens whether we rap about it or not. But when we rap about it, and their children are listening, it's right in their faces. **"**

Snoop, on the U.S. media attitude to gangsta rap music, interview with David Sheff, *Playboy*, October 1, 1995.

"

I'm not rapping, I'm conversing. It's just a conversation between me and you. I'm no reporter. That's for the man with a suit and tie. I'm just relating to my people the best way I know, bringing them what they know and what they see out on the streets. I'm bringing it to them in a musical way, through a way of partying rather than violence. Now they can party their way through their problems.

"

Snoop, on his iconic laidback rap style, interview with David Sheff, *Playboy*, October 1, 1995.

"

My raps are incidents where either I saw it happen to one of my close homies or I know about it from just being in the ghetto. I can't rap about something I don't know. You'll never hear me rapping about no bachelor's degree. It's only what I know and that's that street life. It's all everyday life, reality.

"

Snoop, on rap inspiration, interview with Touré, *New York Times*, January 17, 2008.

"

Tha Doggfather was a rebirth of me, as far as me being more positive on what I was trying to say and trying to live the life through my music, instead of me just living my life, trying to show people that my life… wasn't like my music… I'm not gonna glorify none of this negativity that Death Row wanted me to do. I'm gonna bring a positive side of music.

"

Snoop, on the differences between *Doggystyle* and *Tha Doggfather*, VH1, December 3, 2006.

"

Rapping was the way out of the ghetto for me. I've rapped since I was a boy. First, I would just say other raps and put my name in. Then I was getting to the point where I didn't want to recite anyone else's words. I wanted to do my own shit. When a beat came along, I just started rapping. I was rapping against other motherfuckers at the time. Everybody was running up on me, like, 'Damn, Snoop, that's tight'.

"

Snoop, on his earliest rapping skills, interview with David Sheff, *Playboy*, October 1, 1995.

> "
>
> I was brainwashed. The pressure was on at an early age. I had a job workin' at [supermarket] Lucky's, makin' 'bout eighty dollars a week. I'd be walkin' home after work in tight slacks and see the homeboys around the way flossin'. That's when I felt like I had to make a decision. Sometimes you gotta make those wrong decisions so that you don't make 'em again.
>
> "

Snoop, on getting arrested for dealing cocaine when he was 18. He spent a year in jail and then another four months after violating probation, interview with Pat Charles, *High Times*, October 20, 2020.

66

Weed is the most important element in hip-hop.

99

Snoop, on weed's importance, interview with Pat Charles, *High Times*, October 20, 2020.

"

Everywhere I go around the world people, you know, I sign more *Doggfather* records than any other record I put out. That's the one I sign the most and I'm proud at the thing I did, and the thing is… sometimes you can outgrow your fans.

"

Snoop, on *Tha Doggfather*, and the response to it from fans, *VH1*, December 3, 2006.

"

I went to [youth football] practice high one day and one of the kids said, 'Coach, you smell like my mama's boyfriend,' and I had to check myself. I stopped smoking weed from that day for 180 days straight. And it made me a better coach and a better person. So, every year when I coach football around the kids, I don't smoke, so that's three months out of the year that I do that.

"

Snoop, on his first weed-smoking hiatus in 2002 and being a football coach, interview with Khloe Kardashian, *Complex*, January 19, 2016.

66

A lot of people like to fool you and say that you're not smart if you never went to college, but common sense rules over everything. That's what I learned from selling crack.

Snoop, on his drug-dealing days, interview with Mike Sager, *Esquire*, July 14, 2008.

“

It's a ghetto thing. You know, we have our own little slang that we use in the ghetto, and it becomes our own language and our own lingo.

”

Snoop, on his iconic -izzle language popularized by the rapper, interview by Larry King, *Larry King Live CNN*, March 26, 2010.

In 1989, shortly after graduating from high school, Snoop was arrested for the first time for possession of cocaine with intent to sell.

He was imprisoned for three years.

66

Weed makes you aware of your surroundings. It makes you watch your back. But, most importantly, when dudes smoke together it spreads peace. If they were on cocaine, they'd actually be doin' the shit that they be rappin' about. Cocaine is terrible, man. I used to sell that shit. I know. It's terrible.

99

Snoop, on weed versus cocaine, interview with Pat Charles, *High Times*, October 20, 2020.

"

When the family moved to north Long Beach from the east side, I was 15. That's when I started seeing real gangsta shit. It wasn't just, 'Oh yeah. Little Johnny got killed down the street the other night.' It was like, pow, pow, pow, pow.

"

Snoop, on the first time he saw a shooting, interview with David Sheff, *Playboy*, October 1, 1995.

"

I don't understand how selling weed could go from being the most hated, the most vicious thing that you could do, to now everybody's capitalizing off of it, and they're leaning toward a demographic that can prosper off of it. I went to jail for it. And it's still on my criminal record.

"

Snoop, on the legalization of marijuana, interview with David Gelles, *New York Times*, July 30, 2021.

"

The first time I got high off marijuana was in the seventies, with one of my uncles. My uncle lit one up, and I hit that motherfucker. I was eight or nine years old.

Snoop, on his first taste of weed, interview with Mike Sager, *Esquire*, July 14, 2008.

❝

In the minds of a lot of people, I was the worst Black man ever created.

Snoop, on his media reputation in the 1990s, interview with Ted Chung, *South by Southwest Music Festival Keynote Address*, March 20, 2015.

"
I guarantee that if the government legalized weed, the crime rate would go down. People would just wanna chill. It's better than committin' a crime.

Snoop, on legalizing weed, interview with Pat Charles, *High Times*, October 20, 2020.

> **"**
> I smoked my first blunt with Tupac. I'd never smoked a blunt before. I was smoking joints.
> **"**

Snoop, on his first blunt, interview with Byron Tau, *Politico*, January 9, 2012.

* A blunt is a hollowed-out cigar stuffed with weed, FYI.

> **"**
>
> If you're trying to shoot somebody and this might be the only time you're going to catch him, you ain't gonna let that chance go by. That's the mentality of the streets. If you let that chance go by, he might catch your ass. That's the way we are brainwashed. Instead of jumping out of the car without the gun and talking to him, you have to shoot.
>
> **"**

Snoop, on drive-by shooting mentality, interview with David Sheff, *Playboy*, October 1, 1995.

"

What I try to push and promote is peace through the whole music industry. I have been in beefs and wars with rappers and conflicts with people but to be the bigger man is to end it. We don't want another tragedy like Biggie or Tupac – we don't need that in hip-hop right now.

"

Snoop, on squashing beefs, interview with Ashahed M. Muhammad, *Final Call*, August 13, 2010.

CHAPTER
FOUR

UNCLE SNOOP

In 1996, Snoop beat the rap of his murder charge, allowing the rapper to keep on spittin' stunning rhymes as a free man.

The same year, his second album, *Tha Doggfather*, cemented his celebrity status, sending Snoop from the doghouse to the mansions of Claremont for good, all while never forgetting his roots.

This is Uncle Snoop's time to shine…

66

I'm Uncle Snoop. That's the name I've been given in the industry because I'm like an uncle to all of the rappers whether they are older than me or younger than me and I love giving advice. I try to get all of the rappers on one page of peace, love and just having soul. This music is not made for us to kill each other. It's made for us to make people have a good time, it's a universal language of all people.

99

Snoop, on being a wise uncle to young rappers, interview with Ashahed M. Muhammad, *Final Call*, August 13, 2010.

66

Dr. Dre. Definitely Puffy. Russell Simmons. Quincy Jones and Charlie Wilson are like uncles to me, where they shape and mold the lifestyle of Snoop Dogg, not just the business. Guys that were in my field but were able to jump outside of it and become bigger.

99

Snoop, on his mentors, interview with David Gelles, *New York Times*, July 30, 2021.

> **66**
> What you learn about being a better person from somebody is more important than what you learn business-wise or career-wise.
> **99**

Snoop, on learning to be a better person, interview with David Gelles, *New York Times*, July 30, 2021.

"

Motherfucker don't need
a gun. He needs his smarts.

"

Snoop, on intelligence versus violence, interview with
David Sheff, *Playboy*, October 1, 1995.

66

I was sent to do this by God, so he's not going to put anything on me I can't handle. If death comes to me, that's what he wants me to have. For now, he wants me to keep building and passing on his message. That's what I'm going to do because I'm destined to live and say things.

99

Snoop, on being a messenger for God, interview with David Sheff, *Playboy*, October 1, 1995.

"

Now that I'm more concerned and caring and a father and a husband – it seems the less respect I get.

"

Snoop, on becoming a father, interview with Sophie Heawood, *The Times*, December 4, 2009.

66

I move with the time. Whatever's happening in time, I'm in.

99

Snoop, on going with the flow, interview with David Sheff, *Playboy*, October 1, 1995.

66

My hero is Bruce Lee. That man means the world to me. He was the first guy that I wanted to be like. He was little, he was calm, and he could kick a whole lot of ass.

99

Snoop, on his favorite hero, interview with *Vanity Fair*, January 28, 2022.

66

Coronation Street – I love it. If they call me, I'll do it. I'll play whenever they need. I love the cinematography, acting, the storylines and just the reality.

99

Snoop, on the TV show he'd most like a cameo in, interview with *The Sun*, March 23, 2023.

66

If I had been a straight-A student my whole life and had rapped about Jesus coming back to save us all, I wouldn't get no media. The motherfuckers wouldn't give a fuck about me. But since I'm telling the truth and been through what I'm stressing and know what I'm talking about, I'm a threat – the same way Malcolm and Martin were.

99

Snoop, on being labelled a threat to American values, interview with David Sheff, *Playboy*, October 1, 1995.

"

Who knows, maybe I could run for President one day.

"

Snoop, on politics, interview with Paul Lester,
Melody Maker, February 5, 1994.

"

We started in 2005 in the inner cities in LA. We've graduated over 5,000 kids from Division One college programs. We graduated over 15,000 kids from high school. We sent 20 kids to the NFL. We have Rhodes scholars, firemen, police chiefs, lawyers, dentists, doctors. We have so many professionals that come out of my league that didn't make it in football, but they made it in life.

"

Snoop, on being Coach Snoop and starting a highly successful football league, interview with Elliott Wilson, *GQ*, December 8, 2021.

66

If you don't like my words, go get some gospel shit, or jazz shit or some whiter shit.

99

Snoop, on gangsta rap albums having stickers to warn buyers of its "offensive and threatening" content, interview with David Sheff, *Playboy*, October 1, 1995.

"

The weed doesn't take away;
it's an attribute, an accolade.
It's like Popeye the Sailor Man.
He'd squeeze that can and pop
that spinach and go into work
mode. That's what weed is.
I'm Popeye the Sailor Man,
I live in a garbage can!

"

Snoop, on weed giving him strength, interview with
Luke Bainbridge, *Observer*, April 26, 2015.

"

I got two sides – malice and wonderland. You don't know what's gonna hit you on this one.

"

Snoop, on *Malice in Wonderland* (2009), interview with *Clash Magazine*, January 2009.

66

America is Snoop Dogg. It's no secret, America loves violence, murder, sex. But we love peace and tranquility, too. So, I give you all of that.

99

Snoop, on America, interview with Chris Campion, *Daily Telegraph*, December 4, 2004.

> **"**
> Once I began to have kids and more responsibilities, then I began to live for them. They gave me more of a reason to be here, more of a reason to make music, to tap into my craft, and I love what I do.
> **"**

Snoop, on his children as inspiration and motivation, interview with Elizabeth Day, *The Guardian*, June 19, 2011.

66

I fell in love with her, and I can't fall out of love with her. We're meant to be. That's just what it is. No matter how old she gets, how many changes she goes through physically, I'm connected with her spiritually so that's where our connection lies.

99

Snoop, on his wife, Shante, interview with Elizabeth Day, *The Guardian*, June 19, 2011.

66

I been in the lane for almost twenty years and I'm pretty sure I'm gonna be doing it for another ten. It's good that everyone does their own thang and forces others to step their game up. Competition is a good thing and is definitely needed in hip-hop.

99

Snoop, on the competitiveness of hip-hop artists, interview with *Clash Magazine*, January 2009.

66

Weed makes me feel the way
I need to feel.

99

Snoop, on his love of weed, interview with Mike Sager,
Esquire, July 14, 2008.

66

I make music that sounds good to one person and one person only: Snoop Dogg. If you ain't down with that, then fuck you!

99

Snoop, on the only critic that matters, interview by *Clash Magazine*, January 2009.

66

On a bad day I'll smoke 5–10 blunts. On a good day 25–30.

99

Snoop, on smoking weed, interview by Simon Hattenstone, *The Guardian*, April 6, 2013.

"

We keep hearing about schools getting shot up, venues being shot up, public places being shot up, and we have to address that. Who better to do it than me because I come from the gangsta lifestyle, carrying a gun every day of the week lifestyle?

"

Snoop, on America's gun violence, interview with Simon Hattenstone, *The Guardian*, April 6, 2013.

❝

I wanna thank the people who fought to bring me back into this beautiful country. I feel the emotion, the spirit, the power, it's so different from any other place I've ever been. The only word I can explain it with is… exuberance… You see the love, from the babies to the owner to the maid, there's no in between when it comes to this love over here, they're feelin' Snoop Dogg, you know what I'm sayin'?

❞

Snoop, onstage at Glastonbury Festival, June 27, 2010.

"

My Snoop Lion name was given to me [by a Jamaican Rastafari priest]. I didn't just decide to change it one day. But I ran with it to reflect a more peaceful and positive attitude for my new *Reincarnated* project. The Snoop Dogg name is so connected to hip-hop, and I didn't want to change that. Hip-hop raised me, and I would never turn my back on it.

"

Snoop, on changing his name to Snoop Lion for his 2012 reggae album and film, *Reincarnated*, interview by Kam Williams, *Kam Williams.com*, July 31, 2013.

"

Snoop Lion was necessary – there was a reason for that. I wanted to speak to something different, a more positive side of me. I wanted to stand up to the gun violence and I wanted to do things that represented the spirit of Rastafari, and that's what Snoop Lion was about. Taking a different approach to my life and my music. Snoop Lion helped me grow into a new Snoop Dogg.

"

Snoop, on the origin of the Snoop Lion name change, interview with Luke Bainbridge, *Observer*, April 26, 2015.

"

Sometimes you have to have the
wrong people around you to know
what the wrong people around you
look like and what they act like.
My experience came from having
the wrong people in my business,
to where they didn't benefit me or
didn't teach me anything.

"

Snoop, on the wrong people, interview with David Gelles,
New York Times, July 30, 2021.

66

They killed Martin, they killed Malcolm. You got two Black folks representing us through the Sixties. One of them was for violence, one was against it, and they both are dead. What is that saying? That's saying America doesn't give a fuck about a Black motherfucker.

99

Snoop, on Malcolm X and Martin Luther King Jnr., interview with David Sheff, *Playboy*, October 1, 1995.

CHAPTER
FIVE

ALL GOOD IN THE HOOD

Arise, Sir Snoop! As the dust of a new millennium settled, Snoop found his paws in many different pies, all in the aim to build a snooper-sized business empire, selling everything from peace and love to doggy treats and his own brand of weed, and everything in between.

Snoop, America's first gangsta CEO, had arrived. About fucking time…

"

It's always there. Even when I'm sleepin'. All I dream about is gettin' paid.

"

Snoop, his mind on his money and his money on his mind, interview with Dan Snierson, *Entertainment Weekly*, November 10, 2006.

"

Snoop Dogg.

"

Snoop, when asked "How would you define success?",
interview with Marian Liu, *Seattle Times*, July 17, 2009.

66

I got three kids. Two boys and a girl. You've got to instill the same values in your kids that were put in you, but not be so disciplinary. I feel like my conversation means more to them than just whacking them.

99

Snoop, on how to be a good father, interview with Adam Sandler, *Interview*, April 10, 2012.

"

I started Doggystyle Records
to give back the opportunity
I was given – you know, seek and
find new talent. It feels good to
give it back.

"

Snoop, on his label Doggystyle Records, interview with
Adam Sandler, *Interview*, April 10, 2012.

66

I want to thank me for believing in
me, I want to thank me for doing all
this hard work. I wanna thank me for
having no days off. I wanna thank me
for never quitting. I wanna thank me
for always being a giver and trying
to give more than I receive. I wanna
thank me for trying to do more right
than wrong. I wanna thank me for
being me at all times. Snoop Dogg –
you a bad motherfucker.

99

Snoop, his now-iconic speech at his Hollywood Walk of
Fame ceremony, November 19, 2018.

Snoop's first taste of musical success was setting rhymes to Dr. Dre's debut single, and No.1 hit, "Deep Cover" in 1992. Snoop's chant of "1-8-7 on an undercover cop" (police code for a murdered policeman) is now considered an iconic line in modern music history.

"

Me and Willie Nelson are sitting side by side. We stick our hands in the KFC bucket at the same time and we grab the same piece of chicken. I'm looking at Willie and I'm like, 'That's you, dawg. My bad.' That was like probably one of the greatest moments of my life. Me and Willie grabbing the same piece of chicken.

"

Snoop, on meeting his idol Willie Nelson, interview with Ted Chung, *South by Southwest Music Festival Keynote Address*, March 20, 2015.

66

My older son, Corde, aka Spank, was really my first love. When he was born, it was like my first love was him. I never knew about those kinda feelings and shit before.

99

Snoop, on the birth of his first child, interview with Mike Sager, *Esquire*, July 14, 2008.

66

As a Black man, you definitely have to be cocky, but not conceited. You got to have that kind of swagger, 'cause there's so much against you, and there's so many people that's just as good as you, if not better than you. You gotta push a little harder to make yourself shine.

99

Snoop, on having swagger, interview with Mike Sager, *Esquire*, July 14, 2008.

Snoop's *-izzle* slang has been widely popularized by the rapper, who can often be found pontizzleficating his catchphrases, such as "Dizzle fo shizzle mah nizzle fo rizzle", "Tinseltown, Fo Shizzle Dizzle it's off the Hizzle" and "Doggy Fizzle Televizzle".

This style of slang is called *cant* and was used by African American pimps and jive hustlers in the 1970s. Give it a try next time you order some food: "One large McChizzle and a frizzle."

> "
>
> Did you pay for the version with the kids, the G-rated Snoop Dogg? Or did you pay for the rated-R Snoop Dogg, the one the adults like? Which one did you pay for? Brands have to accept all of that when you're dealing with Snoop Dogg.
>
> "

Snoop, on the many sides to Snoop Dogg, interview with David Gelles, *New York Times*, July 30, 2021.

"

Last year I got two Adult Video News Awards. Snoop Scorsese, that's my director name.

"

Snoop, on his second career as an adult porn movie director, interview with Adam Sandler, *Interview*, April 10, 2012.

"

Nobody cared about the L.A. riots until they thought it might spill into their nice neighborhoods. When it was in my hood, the police didn't give a fuck. When the looting was going on, the police ran right past. You saw it on TV: Everybody was running out of the stores and the police weren't doing shit. But when it spread to Beverly Hills, the police started beating motherfuckers.

"

Snoop, on the L.A. riots, interview with David Sheff, *Playboy*, October 1, 1995.

66

All of the young Black content creators on TikTok have boycotted because they see that when they do the dances they don't get the attention or the money. But as soon as the white dancers do it, it's the biggest thing in the world. That's not fair. It's not cool to just keep stealing our culture right in front of us and not include us in the finances of it all.

99

Snoop, on racist cultural appropriation, interview with David Gelles, *New York Times*, July 30, 2021.

"

I walk the fine line between the corporate world and the streets. I call it Hollyhood.

"

Snoop, on the two sides of Snoop, interview with Larry King, *Larry King Live CNN*, March 26, 2010.

"

It's got to be fun. And it's going to make funds. So long as the word 'fun' is involved, it's cool.

"

Snoop, on building his business empire and choosing which big brands to work with, interview with David Gelles, *New York Times*, July 30, 2021.

66

I'm a marketing genius and
I can show a new artist a few
things that the labels ain't going
to show you. They're going to
be trying to rob you and rape
you. I'm going to be trying to
build you and shape you.

99

Snoop, on helping new rap artists, interview with
Elliott Wilson, *GQ*, December 8, 2021.

66

We should be able to have some of our people – that look like me – as executives, as C.E.O.s, as platform owners. You know, the top of the chain, not just the spokesperson or the brand ambassador. We need to be the brand owners.

99

Snoop, on trying to close the Black wealth gap in corporate America, interview with David Gelles, *New York Times*, July 30, 2021.

> **"** What makes the most sense to me is me being the 'Black Forest Gump' – seeing me in all of these highlighted moments in American history. **"**

Snoop, on what the Hollywood biopic of his life would be, interview with Lyndsey Parker, *Yahoo Music*, May 10, 2021.

"

I'm trying to be an example of someone who creates his own everything, owns his own everything, and has a brand strong enough to compete with Levi's and Miller and Kraft and all of these other brands that have been around for hundreds of years. That's what I want the Snoop Dogg brand to be.

"

Snoop, on Brand Snoop, interview with David Gelles, *New York Times*, July 30, 2021.

"

I'm just a hustler. I've got the GPS, the Football League, the clothing line, the TV shows, the movie deals. Everything that I do is always about trying to get to the next level, whether it's financially, spiritually, or just mentally.

"

Snoop, on being a hustler in business and life, interview with Larry King, *Larry King Live CNN*, March 26, 2010.

> **"**
>
> I was surprised it took so fucking long. I think Michelle was like, 'It's time to get the Doggfather in here.'
>
> **"**

Snoop, on his historic invitation to meet President Obama at the White House in 2013, interview with Lyndsey Parker, *Yahoo Music*, May 10, 2021.

> **"**
> I don't want to associate myself with people who don't have a like mind as me. Companies that get down with me know how I get down. They know the extracurricular things that I do. They know the things that I do in the hip-hop world and in the business world.
> **"**

Snoop, on collaborators, interview with David Gelles, *New York Times*, July 30, 2021.

"

The more success you have and practice you have with acting, the more familiar you become with it. Either love it or hate. I love what it does for me, and I love what it does for other people when they see me onscreen. It's a feeling of joy when people understand it and they get it.

"

Snoop, on his first attempts at acting, interview with David Gelles, *New York Times*, July 30, 2021.

❝

My greatest achievement? My business portfolio and my kids. I've been able to explore my many passions and interests: making spirits with Indoggo Gin and 19 Crimes, entering the fashion game with my G-Star denim line and Snoopy's Clothing, entering the metaverse with Sandbox, and performing with Dr. Dre at the Super Bowl this year.

❞

Snoop, on his greatest achievements and entrepreneurial success, interview with *Vanity Fair*, January 28, 2022.

"

I earned the right to call my album *Ego Trippin'*. Nine records in 15 years, top 10 every time I come. I earned the right to do that. Fuck whoever don't like it.

"

Snoop, on remaining relevant, interview with Emma Forrest, *The Guardian*, April 3, 2008.

"

It's a blessing to have been in the rap game for so long and to remain so relevant, to remain talked about with the newest and the latest and the hottest, freshest.

Snoop, on remaining relevant, interview with Emma Forrest, *The Guardian*, April 3, 2008.

"

Before social media, I was always up close and personal with the people who would respect my music and love my music. And social media gives me a chance to get even more up close and personal. To have your fan base actually be a part of your life and your family is the key to my longevity because I never separated them. I never put a wall between me and them. I've always kept us in one room.

"

Snoop, on the secret to his success, *XXL Magazine*, January 2014.

"

Talking about myself being shot at is a hard example for little kids. I just want people to understand that those situations do take place, and just because I'm rappin' doesn't mean it can't happen to me. I'm not gonna say on my records, 'Don't do drugs'. I'm gon' say, 'Snoop Dogg did this, Snoop Dogg did that, and it was nothin' nice.' If people are like I was, they can understand what I'm stressin'.

"

Snoop, on being real with his fans, interview with Steven Daly, *The Face*, February 1994.

"

My branding and my business came when I was able to go to No Limit Records with Master P. He taught me how to be a better businessman, how to be more than just a rapper, but to be about my business. It's called show business. I had mastered show. But Master P showed me how to master the business.

"

Snoop, on building a business empire, interview with David Gelles, *New York Times*, July 30, 2021.

CHAPTER
SIX

FO SHIZZLE, MY NIZZLE

For three decades, Snoop Dogg has been beloved as a cartoonish character enjoyed by millions, much like his namesake – full of mischief, imagination, humour and love.

Now, for the final time, let's inhale and get high on Snoop's most classic moments and hope that for the next 30 years, he'll take us to even higher heights…

66

I don't represent the Democratic party, I don't represent the Republican party, I represent the motherfucking gangsta party!

99

Snoop, on politics, interview with Luke Bainbridge, *Observer*, April 26, 2015.

> **"**
>
> In hip-hop, we weren't taught we could grow old. When we were young, 50 was old. Fifty was an old man in a wheelchair, talking shit, eating peanuts, and throwing shells on the porch all day. Our 50 is different. Our 50 is agile. Our mind is there, we sharp, we still got the will to win, and we hate to fucking lose. Even at 50.
>
> **"**

Snoop, on turning 50 in 2021, interview with Elliott Wilson, *GQ*, December 8, 2021.

66

Rock and roll don't have no age on it. Don't nobody ever say, 'The Rolling Stones is 80 years old. Them old motherfuckas need to sit down somewhere.' They say, 'The Rolling Stones is doing a stadium concert!' It needs to be the same for hip hop, for rap.

99

Snoop, on old age in rap music, interview with Elliott Wilson, *GQ*, December 8, 2021.

66

My dream is to go on vacation for five years straight and have so much shit out there that you don't even know that I'm on vacation. I never had a vacation since I was in the music industry. Never, not once.

99

Snoop, on taking a break from all his businesses and brands, interview with Elliott Wilson, *GQ*, December 8, 2021.

"

She stayed down for the get-down;
she stayed down for the come-up.
I put her through so much shit being
with me, holding on with me, all
the bullshit I put her through. She
remained rock solid the whole way
through, so that's how you repay
people for being solid and being
loyal. You cut them into it, and now
it's theirs.

"

Snoop, on making Shante, his wife, his manager, interview
with Elliott Wilson, *GQ*, December 8, 2021.

66

There was one point in time when I didn't care nothing about nothing but my music and my life and my shit, and fuck everything else. Selfish. Now I'm selfless.

99

Snoop, on becoming a better Snoop, interview with Elliott Wilson, *GQ*, December 8, 2021.

81

According to Snoop himself, in a 2013 Tweet, the most amount of blunts smoked by the rapper in one day.

"

I stay ready so I ain't gotta get ready. I'm a musician – I'm always making music.

"

Snoop, on remaining prolific, interview with *Clash Magazine*, January 2009.

66

I was given the power, the position. I know it's my job to uphold hip-hop for all the right reasons. To stand up, be political and to be rational at times as well. So, I accept my responsibility and I know my role.

99

Snoop, on knowing his role within hip-hop, *XXL Magazine*, January 2014.

"

That's why I'm so universally accepted when it comes to music, because I listened to everybody's music as a kid. I grew up with rock music, rap music, reggae music and whatever sound was in my neighbourhood.

"

Snoop, on his universal musical influences, interview with Steve Baitlin, *Billboard*, June 17, 2019.

Rollin' 20s Crips

The name of Snoop's former gang in Long Beach, West Los Angeles, California.

"

I feel like a Malcolm X figure now. But, you know, a lot of times little white kids come up to me, and it makes me feel damn good. Sometimes I ask them if they really listen to the tape, and they know every word. I'm not prejudiced in my rap; I just kick the rhymes.

"

Snoop, on white kids listening to gangsta rap, interview with Jeff Rosenthal, *Rolling Stone*, July 31, 2012.

> "
>
> I felt like I was out of pocket. I apologized to him, and I let him know and I'm just bettering myself. I make mistakes. I ain't perfect. I'm Snoop Dogg.
>
> "

Snoop, on squashing his infamous beef with Dr. Dre's newest protegé, Eminem, interview with DJ Envy, *The Breakfast Club*, May 18, 2018.

147

Snoop's reported IQ, which is indicative of a talented genius.

If accurate – and we must assume it is considering all of his music and business savvy – Snoop is much, much cleverer than the average dog, which has an IQ of around 100.

> **"**
> Man, when I got home and
> watched it on playback,
> I thought it was the greatest shit
> ever. Being there it felt like the
> greatest concert of all time.
> **"**

Snoop, on performing with Dr. Dre at the Super Bowl
LVI Halftime Show in 2022, interview with Elliott Wilson,
TIDAL Magazine, March 4, 2022.

"

Snooperman goes in the booth and gets it done. Clark Kent ain't got shit on me. I write about the shit I see, been through and what I'm about to do. There's no formula to it – just timeless music.

"

Snoop, on his rapping abilities, interview with *Clash Magazine*, January 2009.

"

Just to break the chain was the key, to be able to say, 'OK, just because I didn't have my father in my life doesn't mean I'm not going to be in my kids' life. I'm going to try my best to be there for them, and if I can't, it's not because I didn't try. '

"

Snoop, on being there for his children (and breaking the cycle), interview with Elizabeth Day, *The Guardian*, June 19, 2011.

"

My DNA is hip-hop. So, if you check my DNA, it got Slick Rick, it got Ice Cube, and it got Rakim. It's so diverse with hip-hop that when Dr. Dre was able to take me and put me on the record with him, anybody that loved and respected hip-hop, had to get down with the get down.

"

Snoop, on having hip-hop in his veins, interview with Elliott Wilson, *CRWN*, August 8, 2016.

> **"**
> You know what, it's kind of like an out-of-body experience.
> I walk around with it, so it's hard for me to look at it. I can't really bask in none of that shit when I'm so steadily trying to make some new shit.
> **"**

Snoop, on what it's like to have a hit song, as well as a catalogue of hit songs, interview with Steve Baltlin, *Billboard*, June 17, 2019.

"

I wouldn't give a fuck about a lot of people being disappointed! Who are a lot of people? I ain't never met them!

"

Snoop, on disappointment, interview with Nima, *Dubcnn.com*, January 2007.

> **"**
>
> All my experiences, talents, wins, and loses, make me who I am today. I am constantly evolving, learning, and working toward not just being great, but also staying true to who I've always been – just a kid with a big dream from the LBC.
>
> **"**

Snoop, on staying true to Snoop, interview with *Vanity Fair*, January 28, 2022.

"

Ain't nothing stopping me.
I've been doing this shit before
I had a record deal, homie!
Muhammad Ali is the greatest
of all time. I'm the greatest of
my time.

"

Snoop, on being the greatest, interview with Nima,
Dubcnn.com, January 2007.

"

I love being high, but I don't like being up high.

"

Snoop, on his only fear – heights, interview with
Vanity Fair, January 28, 2022.

66

My goal is just to see hip-hop continue to grow. I know I'll be in the Hip-Hop Hall of Fame by then 'cause they'll have one by then. Rock & Roll Hall of Fame, maybe. Somewhere kickin' it, chillin'. Still doing shows but in Las Vegas on the residency tip with a bunch of old folks in the crowd rockin' with me.

99

Snoop, on his goals for the future, *XXL Magazine*, January 2014.

"

Sometimes, when we get big, like I am, we don't have anybody that we can turn and talk to. That leads us to get caught up in crazy shit. But I have good friends around me now who understand what I'm going through and help put me back on the right page.

"

Snoop, on staying grounded, interview with Chris Campion, *Daily Telegraph*, December 4, 2004.

"

As a gangsta ass football coach who loved his family and kids and did tha best at everything he did and didn't take shit from no one, ya dig?

"

Snoop, on how he'd like to be remembered, interview with Rosanna Greenstreet, *The Guardian*, November 28, 2009.

66

I love the haters because it means I'm doin' good, but it sucks that they gotta hate, ya dig?

Snoop, on his haters, interview with Rosanna Greenstreet, *The Guardian*, November 28, 2009.

66

Hip-hop fans are true. If you come with the bomb and keep comin' with the bomb, they gon' stay down wit' you. But if you come with the bullshit, it'll be like you're startin' all over again.

99

Snoop, on hip-hop fans, interview with Steven Daly, *The Face*, February 1994.

"

Don't change a motherfuckin'
thing.

"

Snoop, when asked to give his younger self any
advice, interview with Lyndsey Parker, *Yahoo Music*,
May 10, 2021.

> **"**
> I believe that rap is the most important form of music right now, because it's the change and the choice of the new generation.
> **"**

Snoop, on the revolution of rap music, interview with Larry King, *Larry King Live CNN*, March 26, 2010.

"

People always get information on me as far as when I go to jail and my criminal record. Negative things. They never hear about my football team, my wife, my kids, my standing in the community, the gang interventions that I do. They don't give a fuck about it!

"

Snoop, on remaining relevant, interview with Steven Daly, *The Face*, February 1994.

"

The easiest thing you can do is just do you. I felt like doing me would be the easiest path to me remaining relevant in the industry. It's originality and uniqueness. I just try to do me.

"

Snoop, when asked "How have you managed to stay relevant for so long?", interview with David Gelles, *New York Times*, July 30, 2021.

" I am my happiest when creating, whether I am in the studio recording my next song, onstage performing in front of my fans, on the football field coaching kids in my Snoop Youth Football League, or on set filming. **"**

Snoop, on when he is at his happiest, interview with *Vanity Fair*, January 28, 2022.